Where the Big Rivers Run

Poems by Doug Washer

Kansas City Spartan Press Missouri

Spartan Press
Kansas City, Missouri
spartanpresskc.com

Copyright (c) Doug Washer, 2018
First Edition 1 3 5 7 9 10 8 6 4 2
ISBN: 978-1-946642-43-1
LCCN: 2018934195

Design, edits and layout: Jason Ryberg
Cover image: Doug Washer
Author photo: Dee Washer
All rights reserved. No part of this publication may be reproduced or transmitted in any form or by any means, electronic or mechanical, including photocopying, recording or by info retrieval system, without prior written permission from the author.

Spartan Press would like to thank Prospero's Books, The Fellowship of N-finite Jest, The Prospero Institute of Disquieted P/o/e/t/i/c/s, Will Leathem, Tom Wayne, Jeanette Powers, j.d.tulloch, Jon Bidwell, Jason Preu, Mark McClane, Tony Hayden and the whole Osage Arts Community.

CONTENTS

Songs for Lola

The Night Watchman / 1

My Lady in Light and Shadow / 2

Lola's Song / 3

Awake in the Night / 4

The Shade of the Stoic Emperor Marcus
   Aurelius Appears to Dee Washer in
   Independence, Missouri / 5

Epitaph / 6

Missing by Inches / 7

When She Leaves Our Bed / 8

Encouragement / 9

Love and Time / 10

I Become Desire / 11

Since Our Breath is Soul / 12

Romance / 13

The Cherry Blossoms / 14

My Baby is a Moon Baby / 15

My Woman is a Little Woman / 16

Night Moment / 17

Married Love / 18

Relativistic Effects / 19

You Are Warm / 20

Warm Rain Laves the Skin of the World / 21

We Played at Love / 22

Credo / 23

For Delores in Spring / 24
Waking From Dreams of Doing Things
  I Pray I'll Never Do / 25
I Say You Are Lovely / 26
Animus / Anima / (1) Animus 27
(2) Anima / 28
Lascaux, 18000 B.C. / 29
Uruk, 4000 B.C. / 30
Troy, 1200 B.C. / 32
Kansas City, Missouri, USA, now / 34
Kansas City, Missouri, USA, 1983-1988 / 35
Independence, Missouri, USA, 1999-present / 37
Dusky Rose / 38

Where the Big Rivers Run

Dancehall Moon / 40
Yesterday I Saw My Breath / 43
Hawk Claws the Power Line / 44
There is a Green That Comes Upon
  a Summer's Day, / 45
As the Night Freezes / 46
In the Tilting Light of the Late Summer Sun, / 47
Kendra's Song / 48
I Would Be a Tree Again: / 49
The Wild Geese Fly South, / 50

Enki / 51
Borges Speaks / 52
My Sister Called, / 53
In a Dream I Came Upon a River
   That I Knew, / 54
Under Summer Moons, / 55
Oh, Young Cicada, / 56
The Sky Cracked, / 57
Dying in Summer, / 58
Momma, if You're Dead, / 59
My Mother Died Twice, / 60
Momma, Your Hair is Growing / 61
Minnie / 62

For Lola

Songs for Lola

The Night Watchman

You cry out from a nightmare's far place,
voice of a child lost so long
the yellow image of the open door
begins to fade.

Cradling your body,
I lure you back with ritual incantation;
soul shocks home: falcon to the falconer's fist.

Lying in the murmuring dark
we share a world
until you turn back to your labyrinth
with its Prince and its Minotaur.

Gathering you like mist
in the net of my arms
I listen.

My Lady in Light and Shadow

Sorrow sits on her shoulder,
Dark Familiar,
purring liquid insinuations of dread and death
into her helpless ear.

Then joy fires her soul,
As the sun dapples brook water fleeing shadow wood.

She shimmers, she shines,
radiant with the light of her own sweet burning.

Lola's Song

Sorrow is not Fire,
for all flames are happy.

Sorrow is not Stone,
for stone knows no lack.

Sorrow is not Wind,
for air is never heavy.

Sorrow must be Water,
seeping through the bone.

Awake in the Night

awake in the night
I listen for your breathing
bless you sleeping there

The Shade of the Stoic Emperor Marcus Aurelius Appears to Dee Washer in Independence, Missouri

Friend, remember:
when the fiercest storm raves,
bending and breaking the tall trees,
tossing the great ships upon the land,
forcing your vision back into the curve of your own eyes,
even then, above all tumult,
the eternal stars never cease in their shining.

Rise, and be free.

(For Valentine's Day, 1997)

Epitaph

We sleep or we rise:
If we sleep, we sleep together,
If we rise, we rise rejoicing.

Missing by Inches

missing by inches
I reach out to stroke your back
as you leave our bed

When She Leaves Our Bed

when she leaves our bed
all the blankets in the house
can't replace her warmth

Encouragement

It must hurt the caterpillar
to leave its tiny room.
But when it's free and flying
do you think the butterfly
ever misses the cocoon?

Love and Time

the rain sound stopped
then started up again
after we made love

I Become Desire

I become desire
flame in the arms of my wife—
words can not say that

Since Our Breath is Soul

since our breath is soul
we are a single spirit
sleeping face to face

Romance

A slender brown woman
stands atop the highest peak of a high mesa,
a place intimate with sun and moon.

This plateau is many colors of earth and rock,
and the brown of the woman, the brown of her eyes,
is one of the colors of the mesa.

The wind always blows here.
It flows around her body like a second skin, clinging,
longingly drawing with its tiny hands her thick dark hair.

She is still, watching like a deer,
as if her life depends upon it.
She has watched while one sun and one moon
crawled across the sky,
watched while distance and dream became a shape
coming ever clearer,
drawn to the steady beating of her heart
and the endless patience of her eyes
(now mirroring unseen a hawk circling in a cloudless sky).

She watches inexorably ride on her blue eyed lover.

The Cherry Blossoms

The cherry blossoms pink and white mass in silence.
A Southern breeze stirs the wind chimes,
sways the blooms in ponderous majesty.
Petals stream away as if upon water.
Chimes fade, blossoms shiver into stillness.

(April, 2006)

My Baby is a Moon Baby

My Baby is a Moon Baby
She rises and falls like the tide
When she dances I dance with her
I hold her tight when she cries

My Baby is a Moon Baby
Like the moon she waxes and wanes
We feast at the tables of plenty
We cry at the tables of pain

My baby is a Moon Baby
She gleams in the silvery light
Great are our pleasures in sunshine
Greater our pleasures at Night

My Woman is a Little Woman

My woman is a little woman
but she's all woman for all that.

The womanliness of a woman
is not measured by the height of her hat!

Night Moment

rain in the drainpipes
one bird repeating two notes
you asleep close by

Married Love

As we sail your splendid ship,
a bird calls outside our window.

It must be a gull,
crying that even on this vast and trackless sea
we will come at last to a landfall
that we know.

Relativistic Effects

When you touch me and touch me and touch me
I spin like a child's go round
absorbing pulses of energy
expanding at the speed of light
shifting to the red behind my eyes
until I touch the universe's rim
turning
imploding upon myself
spiraling toward the core
collapsing to infinite density
becoming for a moment nothing
appearing in another time and space delighted
to find you
still
there

You Are Warm

You are warm beneath your breasts
where their rounded fullness rests
and your mouth is hot and sweet
but oh the fierce transforming heat
where your fine legs do rise and meet

Warm Rain Laves the Skin of the World

Warm rain laves the skin of the world
as a man's hand will trace
the curve of his lover's buttocks.

Just green trees are skinny girls,
their buds stiffen like nipples under
the knowing hands of the breeze.

Turning from the window, I find Africa in my bed.

Naked and steaming from your bath,
colors of copper and earth and obsidian,
you are a land of elemental wonders.

I come into your valleys as a thunderstorm,
wedded to you by lightning,
changed by you into a mountain lake.

A mountain lake over which you bend,
mirrored, the masked perfection of your face.

We Played at Love

We played at love upon the bottom of the lake;
then the gills bloomed like coral at our throats.
When we bedded down upon fronds, the fish watched,
ranged about us in circles, eyes goggling.

The moon fell, silver apple from the tree of night.
Its great bulk entered the water without a sound.
We swam up through the moon, water made milk,
up to where the dark wind feasted upon our faces.

The moon's rays held us up; we danced swaying in the water,
our legs intertwining, our mouths touching.
From our murmuring a heron was born—it winged away.

Credo

The balm of breeze upon the brow
is all we know of Gilead,
the cool of water in the throat
is what we call God's love.
The ease of sleep when we lie down
is all there is of heaven,
the touch of bodies in the dark
is our paradise.
There is no Watcher in the Hills,
the hills watch us alone,
behind the features of this world
there lies only stone.

We are gods bound by our own hands,
and by our hands are freed,
to sow our souls among the stars
like suns strewn out for seed.

For Delores in Spring

By the bridge,
from the river's margin,
newly green trees lift up
still skeletal fingers,
dappled with buds;
a ritual gesture,
endlessly repeated,
I begin to understand.

Waking From Dreams of Doing Things
I Pray I'll Never Do

Waking from dreams of doing things I pray I'll never do,
with an erection like a golden railroad spike
bound for the Continental Divide to nail two halves
of a country together,
I long to wake you up.
But you sleep defenseless as a child,
and I am not sure who I really am.

I Say You Are Lovely

I say you are lovely, graceful in your movements,
delightful in the very being of your sweet body.
I say there is no harm in you, no hate, and that
children love you because you pity the powerless.
I say you are a flame in my arms, a flame in which I
perish eagerly, rising stronger and more real.
I say you know darkness and suffering but struggle
bravely and without ceasing to live in the light and in joy.
These things are true, but cannot capture you—
you escape my words as the real moon forever transcends
the moons of all the poets.
But words are all I have.

You are a scent upon the night wind— mysterious, subtle,
disturbing, entwining and suffusing, light as air and
binding as Fate— my Fate, my Love.

But these too are only words and I go on seeking in the
foolish, foredoomed quest of poets and lovers.

Animus / Anima

(1) Animus

You don't know me face to face
but I have loitered with intent among the shadows
of your dreams.

I am Joshua come to bellow down your mighty walls
and fix a merciless eye upon your inward city.

I am the shaman doctor in his tower
discarding petal after petal of accidental ego
seeking the eternal Woman in you.

I am Theseus threading your labyrinth
killing the monster god
leaving you to preside over your own altar.

I have come to save you from the hell of a diminished
life having bought you with my song
and I listen with all my soul
for your footsteps at my back.

It is Orpheus, Eurydice.

(2) Anima

Two sides of a single mask
we can never show just one face
except in spinning blurred,
but in the darkness
when you're still
I am the woman's voice you hear
telling stories.

Lascaux, 18000 B.C.

I hunker solid on my haunches
gourd belly swollen ripe.
Facing, you squat brown and sinewy
as when I first chose you amazed
eyes worshiping.
Muscles in my womb knot and smooth
knot and smooth
like your arms rowing into me
heaving spent upon my shore.
Sweating and shuddering I thrust our child through
the slit between the worlds.
You sit animal still gripping the stone goddesses
one in each hand
all belly and breast and buttock
like me.

Uruk, 4000 B.C.

Holy Inanna, Queen of Heaven and Earth,
hear your High Priestess.
So old now only you share my memories
your dark sister dispatches her demons from the
Great Below bearing my death.
The necklace of my life is broken.
I live in dreams of long ago
when you toppled Gilgamesh the giant cedar
in your windstorm,
breaking him for spurning you,
sinning as man, and Priest, and King.
His was the inconsolable sobbing of an orphaned child
when the brother I brought him from the steppes died.
Enkidu raised his head from the pool
when I appeared naked before him.
I brought his hand to my breasts
and the wetness between my legs,
his eyes glazed, he thrust like a bull.
Six days and seven nights he rode me.
Under that heaving avalanche my mind
broke its moorings,
I drifted to the future.
I saw his death, the King's, my own.
And then, First daughter of the Moon, I saw a time
when the eternal gods no longer gather like flies
to the sacrifice.

I saw a terrible god come with no woman in him.
My vision failed.
Do not hate me for telling you this.
You will again be worshipped in the land.
As for me, I have been faithful and will be faithful even after death,
in the Dark Kingdom of your sister, your foe.

Troy, 1200 B.C.

Stranger, why do you walk along this dark
and misty shore?
I watch the sea, waiting for the ships
to appear against the fog.
The net of the universe knots in me,
I can feel the warriors coming,
though Apollo has seen that no man heeds.
You turn your face, believing I am mad.
It is the god who does this,
spitting in my mouth again.
He loved me from childhood, when his sacred
serpents licked my ears as I slept
on the cool stones of his altar.
When he came for me, I was only afraid,
only afraid, a girl needing to be wooed.
But in his anger and his pride he cursed me.
Now the future holds no fear for me.
I have seen my city burned,
scried my mother's slavery and my own.
I have seen my father's butchering and my own.
My vision is a hawk, widening in its gyre until
freedom takes it unaware.
I see my revenge, a time
when Apollo is but a name and voiceless winds
blow through the ruins of Delphi.

Look, Stranger, how the sun fires the wine dark sea.
Why do you stare at me that way?
I know you can't believe me.
Ah, it's you.
Tell me, Phoebus, how do you like your dawn?

Kansas City, Missouri, USA, now

My husband is beginning to remember who I am.
He fears I may be evil, hissing back over my shoulder,
cracking the bone with my teeth, seeking the marrow.
Our bed is a foxes' den, smelling always just faintly
of blood, and my eyes glitter from its shadow.

At night I crawl upon him, crouching like a Sphinx
shivering down upon his cock.
I rear up like a puppet with his hand inside me,
swaying and keening.

I come in a blaze of silence, ebbing to a gibbous moon,
smeared with his seed.

When I fall from that high place, coiling upon myself,
he pulls me to him as a hand grasps a thistle.

Soon I will tell him my name.
I am your Lilith, my Adam.

Kansas City, Missouri, USA, 1983-1988

Dreaming lifted up a tree
to show a child the full moon's world.

River curving like an eye,
lovers lush among its lashes,
a coalblack mare grazing silver grasses
freezes the boy in her golden gaze.

He starts awake from a dream of falling,
faintly hears his mother calling,
scrambles down to find his home.

His house is pouring yellow light
from every window and every door,
and yellow is the color of love
so the boy goes to the night no more.

You were the tree,
and you were the river,
you were the moon,
and you were the mare;
we were the lovers lying together,
I was the boy with the wide-eyed stare;
you were my house,
and you were my mother,

you were the light the color of love;
you were my dream,
and you are my waking;
inside your scent I will make me my home.

Independence, Missouri, USA, 1999-present

I said: *I am an orphan now that Momma's dead.*

You said: *I will be your mother.*

I lost the angel you gave me, I said, *I must have dropped it from my pocket.*

I will be your angel, you said, releasing your light.

(end of Animus/Anima)

Dusky Rose

My dusky rose,
the sweetest flower that grows.
Those other roses only fade,
your beauty only grows.

Where the Big Rivers Run

(For my mother and father)

Dancehall Moon

Daddy came to the dancehall,
saw his dream move on the floor.
Said to the men around him:
I aim to dream that dream some more!
Drove her home from the dancehall,
the moon was wild and free,
drove her home from the dancehall
and that was the start of me.
That was the start of my brothers
and of our sister surprise.

Love's a knot in living ordinary lives,
as constellations cast their nets upon the skies.

Momma came to the funeral home,
saw an old man lying there.
Cried, *what's become of my Dancehall Man
and all that golden hair?
What's become of my Dancehall Man
who shone beneath the moon?
He gave me the twenty years he had,
but twenty years came too soon.*

Death's a knot in living ordinary lives,
as constellations cast their nets upon the skies.

Momma walked to the graveyard,
the moon shone on the stone,
whispered *Daddy, can I go on living,*
so lonely and so lone?
Daddy, can I go on living?
But she waited for that day,
she wouldn't walk to the graveyard
and she wouldn't walk away.

Grief's a knot in living ordinary lives,
as constellations cast their nets upon the skies.

My babies came to this world by two
and they came much too soon.
One was round and buttery beneath the birthing moon;
one was round and buttery, the other hid a flaw inside,
Within her heart the doctors said, *a knot must be retied.*
So they stretched her on a table when she was only three
and I froze with fear until they gave my baby whole to me.

Oh, Joy's a knot in living ordinary lives,
as constellations cast their nets upon the skies.

I came to music late and slow,
my music took me deep.
I see the shadow side of things,
I listen while I sleep.

I see the shadow side of things beneath
the dancehall moon,
I know now it's the silence we use to make the tune.

A poem's a knot in living ordinary lives,
as constellations cast their nets upon the skies.

Yesterday I Saw My Breath

That splendid barbarian Winter returns slowly from
his palace in the North, driving the birds before him.
They rest here, filling the trees to bursting and more
than bursting, making the trees more than trees,
cacophonous minds of angels or demons,
angels I think, there's no harm in them.
Soon they will be gone, leaving the trees less than
trees, bereft of birds and leaves and life and hope.
We shall miss them, studying the skies,
gazing down the long lines of their going.
We shall miss too those other souls,
those other souls who have left us to face this Winter
alone, those other souls who will not be returning.

Hawk Claws the Power Line

dividing the world.
Live prey before,
dead past behind.
Like us, like time.

There is a Green That Comes Upon a Summer's Day,

at dusk or before the storm,
a green not just of grass or leaf but of the very air,
in which we pause suspended,
dissolving in darkness, or in rain.

As the Night Freezes

liquid panes of rain shatter—
Summer's luck is gone

In the Tilting Light of the Late Summer Sun,

the boys from the Art Institute gather on their balcony
to talk and paint.
Taking the brush by turns they dream together
a common beauty.
One paints, legs akimbo, the others brace against the
vortex of light flowing into the canvas like an eye.
When night shows the other face of their god,
they fade through a darkening doorway.
From which later, still watching, I hear music and see
yellow light.

Kendra's Song

After Daddy left, Momma drove us kids cross country
to Kansas where she had kin.
It was rough but not all bad.
To get clean we washed in a tub by the stove in Winter.
In Summer, we took shower baths, then rode like
crazy round the yard,
stark naked on our monkey bikes.

I Would Be a Tree Again:

fissuring far out as in,
netting both earth and sky;
silent, silent as the rocks, the stars,
giving no sound not evoked by wind or axe
or lightning stroke,
mute as a guitar;
patient, patient as the sea,
seven her caresses, never more and never less,
upon the sandy belly of the world;
forgotten, a tree among bare trees,
past sins of my life forgiven,
my leaves upon the leaves;
and as the ice lets go the land,
I would be a man again.

(in Norse mythology, humans were originally trees)

The Wild Geese Fly South,

their harsh cries tear at my heart—
where has my life flown?

The wild geese return,
They sleep tonight on home waters—
I will start again.

Enki

I am the god of those deep waters
shoaling darkly over rock that has not
and will not ever see the sun.
Rising in that stony grip,
issuing in places both secret and well seen,
I bear a message to every creature that water needs:
great gods lie downward as well.
Then falling, falling through a labyrinth of ways,
closing a circle older than the grave.

(Enki was the Sumerian god of sweet, i.e. not salt, water. He was a friend to Man.)

Borges Speaks

I am nearly blind now having spent
all the colors but one through innumerable acts
of staining the things of this world.
Chestnut and grey, sorrel and roan, those horses
of my youth, blue black masses of woman's hair,
mazes of ink down all the white pages—
these have exacted their price.
I have saved only yellow, casting about me a charmed
circle of flickering dream.
This too begins to fade.
My soul turns its back on the world.
I find myself already in a place
where eyes are as useless as the shed skins of serpents.

My Sister Called,
(for Connie)

Saying they had torn down the house of our childhood,
built by Daddy and his men from lumber they had milled.
Now, she said, the corn grows right up to the road.

In a Dream I Came Upon a River That I Knew,

although my eyes had never seen that stream before.
It was lovely in its flowing, glacially slow,
and glowing with the inward light of souls.
Kneeling in the shallows,
leaning on fists white as fishes,
throwing my long hair before me,
I lowered my ear to the skin of the current,
listening as my hands froze,
listening as my hair became a twisted clotted mane,
listening to the voices of my dead.

Under Summer Moons,

we played at Hide and Seek—
I have not been found.

Oh, Young Cicada,

Now your call is high and shrill—
Summer hoarsens all.

The Sky Cracked,

The day my brothers told me
told me Daddy's death.

Dying in Summer,

Daddy said something that way,
how ripeness is loss.

Momma, if You're Dead,

How can you come back to me,
sharp as the tang of vinegar?

My Mother Died Twice,

once by drink and once in the usual way.
The first more dreadful she lingered like the
malevolent new dead of primitive peoples.
Risen by my sister's iron love and her own Tennessee
hill woman stubbornness,
she never quite became the woman who raised us.
Only of course to die the second time.
I don't trust her now.
Momma, you old shapeshifter,
what further adventures of transformation
do you enjoy?

Momma, Your Hair is Growing

in the field where you lie sleeping,
long and lush like the other grasses.
Not from ashes to ashes do we pass
but from seed to fruit and flower
and back to seed again
when our brief hour beneath the sun is run.

Minnie

My grandmother was mean when young,
my mother said, but when I knew her,
time and blindness had leached the fierceness away.
She planted flowers in coffee cans and would always
have beauty around her,
even beauty she could no longer see.
In her great old age, she knew no one,
but just before dying she came back to herself and
called her daughter's names:
said STELLA MAE, said BONNIE, said ARDELLA,
said MATTIE, and knew their voices.

She was sweet to me, she was sweet to me,
and made the only chicken and dumplings
there will ever be.

Doug Washer was born and raised in Southeast Missouri on a farm and attended a one room school house located on that farm for the first eight grades. He graduated from Charleston High School then attended what was then Southwest Missouri State College, graduating with the first B.A. in Philosophy awarded by that institution. He earned a Master's degree in Philosophy from the University of Missouri / Columbia before entering the United States Air force for four years. Upon leaving the USAF he began teaching Philosophy and other disciplines in the greater Kansas City area, including eleven years for Park University and twenty for Longview Community College. At the latter school, he received the Governor's Award for Excellence in Teaching, an award of which he is especially proud because it was voted by his peers. He has written poetry for some thirty years and is now working on a novel. He is married to his true love and has grown children, grandchildren, and great-grandchildren.

This project was made possible, in part, by generous support from the Osage Arts Community.

Osage Arts Community provides temporary time, space and support for the creation of new artistic works in a retreat format, serving creative people of all kinds — visual artists, composers, poets, fiction and nonfiction writers. Located on a 152-acre farm in an isolated rural mountainside setting in Central Missouri and bordered by ¾ of a mile of the Gasconade River, OAC provides residencies to those working alone, as well as welcoming collaborative teams, offering living space and workspace in a country environment to emerging and mid-career artists. For more information, visit us at www.oac.com

Osage Arts Community

www.ingramcontent.com/pod-product-compliance
Lightning Source LLC
Chambersburg PA
CBHW021449080526
44588CB00009B/758